THE POSITIVE SIDE

By: Melinda Green-Carpenter

The Positive Side

Copyright © 2020 by Melinda Green-Carpenter

ISBN: 9798632794794

Imprint: Independently published

All rights reserved. Except for use in any review, the reproduction or use of this work in whole or in part in any form by electronic, mechanical, or other means now known or hereinafter invented, including xerography, photocopying, recording, or in any information storage or retrieval system, is forbidden without the written permission of the authors. Author can be contacted via email at kelinlae@yahoo.com.

First, I would like to thank God for saving my life and giving me the gift to write poetry. Thanks to my husband Keith for always pushing me to be the best me that I can be. To my beautiful daughter Aleese, thank you for inspiring and encouraging me. Thanks Dad, Mom, Shay, Kisha, Rebecca and Mary for always pushing me to write a book and for believing in me when I was lacking faith in myself. Thanks to my family and friends for supporting me and insisting that I write/read poems for different events. Thanks to everyone who is taking the time out to read this. God bless you all.

Melinda

The Positive Side

INTRODUCTION

I remember I used to write poems to share at the club's Poetry Night. Some were seductive, some about love, heartbreak or whatever I was feeling at that time. The owner of the club told me that people used to come from miles just to hear me. I really thought I was doing something. Now I know better. I realize that I was not using the gift that God gave me to glorify Him. God designed me to be who I am. Every gift I have is from Him and now I am using them for His glory. It feels so good to write poetry that I know is pleasing to Him. I'm on the positive side now. I want to share with you some of my life's journey and how I grew to be the woman I am today. Let's take a journey to **The Positive Side**.

My Testimony

I used to feel insecure growing up as a child.

I was so used to my siblings' teasing me, I was even ashamed to smile.

I didn't know how to receive when people called me pretty.

I used to think they just said it out of pity.

When I became a teenager, I gained all kinds of attention

I was so happy to receive what I thought was positive affection.

I started drinking, smoking and clubbing at the age of thirteen

I wanted so much attention; I just had to be seen.

I thought since I was with my sisters, we weren't doing any wrong

We just loved to sing and dance to our favorite songs.

Little did I think, this would become my lifestyle

I developed so many bad habits, while I was still considered a child.

I knew about Jesus and my parents instilled the word in me

They didn't even realize that I was running what I thought was free.

I used to make all A's until the world got my time

Having fun was the only thing, which I had on my mind.

I jumped into so many relationships and dropped them so fast.

My Testimony

I was living so carefree. I didn't really care for them to last.

I worked several jobs but still partied all the time.

I thought my life, was doing just fine.

I remember quitting my job and depending on a Man

Then he became controlling, so I was single once again.

I start bootlegging in the projects, selling liquor, beer and drugs.

I had start hanging out and chilling with all kinds of thugs.

They used to pay for weed and drinks and share it all with me

I thought I was winning, because everything seemed free.

I remember playing my gospel so loud for all my neighbors

Even though I was living wrong I stilled believed in my Savior.

I used to tell my customers, to have a blessed day

Some of them looked at me crazy; they didn't know what to say.

Someone told my Daddy, when he asked, I couldn't lie

You would think I would've stopped after seeing my Daddy cry.

I was caught up in the fast money. I got to party and get paid.

I didn't consider me hurting people, off the money that I made.

My Testimony

When a fight broke out at my home, I finally got put out

It was Jesus saving my life. I know that without a doubt.

I needed to leave that environment, before I would end up in jail.

Or even worse than that, I could have been in Hell.

Well later I got pregnant and I wanted so badly to live right

I start going back to church and trying to be a light.

Then, I developed this skin condition and it had me so depressed

I start back drinking and smoking to help relieve the stress.

Well that led back to partying day after day

I left the church again and let the devil lead me astray.

I backslid so many times year after year

But Jesus never left or forsaken me he always remained here.

Now I know how much he loves me because how he keeps forgiving me

He filled me with His spirit now I can be free

So, I will always praise his name for turning my life around

He is the only one who could pick me up when I was so down.

So even if I mess up, I'll continue to praise Jesus Christ.

My Testimony

He died for all those sins I did, He made the ultimate sacrifice.

No matter what I do, He still has my back.

If I confess and try to do better, He will always pick up my slack.

If you don't have a one on one with Jesus, I recommend you do so.

Without the Savior on your side, you know where you will go.

He will free you from your guilt, shame and all your remorse

Give your life to Jesus; He is the Lord of all Lords!

I see you

I see you over there, acting like you don't care

But deep inside that burden, is getting harder to bear.

Yeah, I can see you too trying to act all tough

While in actuality, your life is really rough.

I see you smiling, just laughing and jokin'

trying to cover up the fact that you're feeling broken

I even see you and all you're trying to do.

Still pushing on after all you've been through.

I see you judging people trying to make them look low

Because you're jealous of them for having a glow

I see you dogging people in your relationships

Because you think one day, they may up and dip

I see drinking and smoking trying to forget

All the pain you have inside and all those regrets

I see you bouncing around looking for love

But you don't realize you have it with your father above.

Yeah that's right! Our father Jesus Christ

He can heal any kind of pain even if you haven't been living right.

I see you

He sees you hurting and just waiting on you to come

He's not worried about any background that you may be from

He's not here to judge, he just wants to be a light

He is the only one who can turn wrongs into rights.

Even when you fall short, time and time again

He'll always be here to hold your hand

Just give him a try and turn from wicked ways

because you may not believe it, but we're in our last days.

Your point of view

You're so pretty, no you look like a freak

You're the strongest woman I know, no you are so weak

You are blessed with wisdom, no you don't have any sense

You are such a peacemaker, no you quick to take defense

You're just the right size, no you are big

I love your natural hair, no you need to wear a wig

You act so classy, no you are too ghetto

You are such a giver, no you just don't know how to say no

Your Spiritual walk inspire me, no you act too Holy

You act nice to everyone, no you're just a want to be

You act so professional, no you want to be white

You always make things happen, no you can't do anything right

You're a great mother, no your child is spoiled

Your life is so peaceful, no you are full of turmoil

All these point of views about little ol' me

They just don't realize that Jesus set me free

Whether you are right or wrong doesn't matter at all

I'll still hold my head up and remember to stand tall.

Opinions

Oh, how the opinions always seem to flow

Who opinion matter is what I really want to know.

They have so many, but which one defines me

If I focused on their opinion where would I be?

Well the good ones I guess is supposed to make me smile.

But if it's a good lie would it still be worthwhile?

I suppose the bad ones is supposed to make me feel down.

But perhaps it's from someone who desires to see me frown.

Sometimes I just laugh when I hear what they say.

I say to myself "Now that one really made my day".

It's a good thing to know who you are in Christ.

If not, you'll probably be seeking anyone's advice

They will offer their opinion 9 times out of 10

Then you'll be so confused because opinions never end.

The thing is everyone thinks they're right

Most don't realize that the Word of God is the real light

That's where you will find the concrete facts

It will tell you who you are and how you supposed to act

If you listen to opinions, you won't make it very far

Read the Bible for yourself, so you will know who you are.

God's Affirmations

Take a moment to think about

The way you view yourself

Our thoughts have power that

can contribute to our overall health.

Do you speak God's affirmations

 over you and your family?

If not, you can be setting yourself up

 for a life full of misery.

We speak from our thoughts that turns into a feeling

And that feeling usually determines how we'll act.

That's why it's so important to think positive

If you want to make a positive impact.

Make a conscious decision to encourage yourself

Even if you're not feeling it at the time.

Those words of life that you speak will begin

 to slowly process into your mind.

Once it's in your mind

You will start to feel brand new.

Trust and believe when you're feeling good

There's no limit to what you can do.

God's Affirmations

If you can't think of anything positive to say

Look to God's Holy word.

There you'll find out who you really are

If you haven't already heard.

God gave you so many gifts and power

Because you're His child that He adores

So, I'm encouraging you to think of His love

but the ultimate decision is still yours.

Purpose

We were all created for a reason

and it's all for God's glory.

So, we must live for a purpose

while walking out our life's story.

Purposely glow in the darkness

By being a shining light.

Purposely try to live a life

That is pleasing in God's sight.

Wake up every morning

With intentions to make someone's day

Let them see the God in you

With your smile or the words, you say.

We were all blessed with gifts

That we can use every single day

So, let's use them with a purpose

So, they won't go away.

We don't have to wait on a special moment

To live life with a purpose

Even if don't feel we reached our destiny

God can still and will use us.

Purpose

We don't know what tomorrow may bring

So, let's live on purpose today.

We can start by simply saying

"Lord, Your Will, Your Way".

Either Or

Either you are living for Jesus or the devil,

You're either walking in the spirit or the flesh.

Either you love your neighbor, or you hate them

You're either walking in joy or sadness.

Either you're being patient or you're anxious

You're either being kind or inconsiderate

You either have good in your heart or evil

You're either thinking positive or negative

Either you're faithful or disloyal

You're either being gentle or harsh

You either have self-control or acting out of control

You're either walking in the light or in the dark

You're either telling the truth or a lie

You either energize or you drain

Either you are bringing peace or bringing drama

You can either cause happiness or cause pain.

Either Or

There's no way around it.

Our actions are either or.

It's important to examine ourselves

To determine who we're really living for.

Heavy Hitters

The time has arrived for us to arise and shine.

We must walk in the power that we were given.

We can't deceive our minds, like things are just fine

While we're losing souls each and every minute.

We must do more, than just talk about a dark force,

We must cancel every assignment from the enemy.

Its time recognize each and every disguise so we can proclaim the victory.

Through intercessory prayer we don't have the burdens to bare because we lift them all up to the Lord.

So, let's get on our knees to help set this world free

You all it's time for us to go to war.

It's time to impact the world, with what we're made of

Because we are the righteousness of Christ

We are no longer enslaved to the enemies' ways

We're about to turn darkness into light.

We are about to do a TKO to every transgression we know

And give a black eye to every lie.

Let's uppercut depression! Using God's word as a weapon

We gonna make sure these demons die.

Heavy Hitters

Guilt will be put to shame at the mention of God's name

We are led by Holy Spirit and we ain't playing no games.

Insecurities and addictions will also have to flee

Because we declare and decree, that we have the victory!

Let's slice all unclean ways with our worship and praise

We Claim joy, peace and love! From our Father above

We're uprooting hatred at the core! So, it can spread no more

We are God's Heavy Hitters and we are going to war!

No More Shame

Someone called it my Glory, but I thought of it as a curse

I guess I allowed my physical features to determine my worth

Someone said God blessed me with this condition because he knew I could handle it with grace

All I could do is wonder why I had to lose the pigment in my face

Yeah it was tough, growing up with dark skin

But I was finally comfortable with the skin I was in

When it started changing, it nearly tore me apart

because when I looked in the mirror, I didn't see my heart

Had I did, I would have said to myself "Lin you are so pretty"

But instead I told myself I'm just a walking mockery

Then here come the haters talking about you must have really been in sin

For God to punish you like this I bet you did something big

Now I'm questioning myself I asked, "God what did I do?"

Haven't I showed you how much I love you?

So many others have done way worse than me

Why do I deserve to live a life of misery?

Some also said, you need to just embrace

I ask, "Would you say that if this was your face?"

No More Shame

I felt like an embarrassment to my friends and family

Like I'm not good enough for them to be seen with me

When I saw others like me, I wondered about their story

Do they feel ashamed or do they consider it as their glory?

The devil had my mind and I was drowning in my tears

He knew that rejection was like one of my fears

I wanted to be accepted and I couldn't see that I was

I only listened to all his lies and didn't think of God's love

I prayed to God to fix me or give me grace

He did and I was able to cope with losing the color in my face.

After accepting myself, here we go again

I loss even more color from my chocolate skin

I'm like what's next?? How far will this go?

Will I end up all white? I really need to know!

Still no answer, but it's okay

I know my God is with me on this trying race.

Understand how we look does not define who we are.

So always shine bright because you truly are a star.

The Storms

So many storms coming from nowhere, it seems like they'll never end.
Just as soon as I make it through one, I notice something forming again.
Some of the storms I must admit, I started them myself.
The rain got so heavy, it left me begging God for help.
When that storm passed it warmed up and like a bird, I started to soar.
I learned from that storm and that's not to start it anymore.
Other storms I have faced, I know was meant to strengthen my Faith.
I'm grateful I know the Lord and I'm covered under His Grace.
Plenty of storms I go through and no one even have a clue.
I feel like there's no reason for me to walk around here looking all blue.
I praised God while He led me through and try to grow at the same time.
There's no need to complain because I always end up just fine.
Some people storms are worse than mine and mines maybe worse than others.
Whether big or small rest assure, God is right here with us.

Why throw Shade

Why do you choose to throw shade my way?
Is that what you believe is going to brighten your day?

No matter if your words are the truth or a lie.
I will always be the apple of my Father's eyes.

What you are doing is dimming your light instead of mine.
Because if I have Jesus, I will always shine.

He's the only one who can give us a glow.
We don't have to walk around trying to put on a show.

We are supposed to use words to edify one another.
it's time to stop throwing shade at your sisters and brothers

Instead of using your energy, trying to dim someone's light
Try focusing on God, and then you too will shine bright.

A Mother's Love

I know in my heart that there's no other

who can compare to the love of a good mother.

A mother's love is sweet, unconditional and pure.

She will give you support in whatever you endure.

She will instill the bible in you to make sure you know

what God's word says and the right way to go.

She will do all she can to put a smile upon your face.

She will continue to pray for you no matter what's the case.

She gets joy out of pouring good seeds into you.

She'll patiently wait to see the harvest that God has for you.

If you ask her advice, she'll be honest with you

Because she knows in her heart, the truth is best for you.

Sometimes it's hard for her to see some things you do

But she'll still trust in God to see you through.

She's not perfect, she also has bad days

But she'll try her best to handle them with grace.

I've been blessed with a strong mother of faith.

She taught us all, that Jesus is the only way.

If you're a mother who fall short on some of the qualities, I named

A Mother's Love

Please understand, there's no need to feel ashamed.

Just stay in the word and continue to pray.

Jesus will be here to show you the way.

So instead of staying up, worrying all night

Give it to Jesus, because he's the way, truth and the life.

To all you Mothers continue to do your best.

Enjoy your Mother's Day and please don't forget to rest.

Fathers Do You Realize

Fathers do you realize, who you really are

And that your child looks at you, like a superstar?

Do you know they hang on to, every word you say?

And just getting your attention, will really make their day?

I hope you understand that you are the leader of their lives

And you are the ones, who is supposed to sacrifice

Do you know you can determine how they feel inside?

And that you are supposed to demonstrate, how to walk with integrity and pride?

Did you know they observe you and try to model what you do?

And sometimes even when you 're wrong, they'll try to take up for you?

Do you know they may think you're right, because they are learning from your ways?

So, understand what you are doing, may be how they behave.

Do you know your child may think that you can handle anything?

And feel like you have more power, than just a human being.

Fathers your children love you and admire you too.

So, make sure you're doing right and leading them to the truth.

Fathers Do You Realize

Don't deceive your children or let them go astray.

They are a gift from God for you to cherish every day.

Father's I hope you realize the best thing for your child's life

Is for to teach them, to have a relationship with Jesus Christ

Today we honor, all the Fathers that try.

You are a very important person, if you didn't realize.

Spread Awareness

Many people don't understand the concept of awareness

They don't see the point of wearing pink and having events

They may not realize the need to be informed.

They probably don't think that they can face the same storm.

People need to know the importance of getting a health screen

That's way more important than looking good on the scene.

Everyone should know that Cancer can affect anyone's life.

Even if you feel like you are living so right.

Early detection is the best way to win.

So please go get checked as if your life really depends.

I hope you all join me is sharing this message.

Let's help crush Cancer by spreading awareness.

Breaking the Silence

Dedicating the month of September to Sickle Cell is a step toward spreading awareness.

Now it's time for us to ask ourselves

What else can I do to break the silence?

You see so many people are living with this painful disease

and some are not here to share their story.

But it seems like when it comes to Sickle Cell

not too many people seem to worry.

It's not because they don't care

I believe they're just not too informed

But their lack of knowledge about this disease

has potential to cause them harm.

Not knowing the facts can stop us from early detection and perhaps prevention.

So, it's time to learn, share, grow and prepare

from this valuable information.

Now let's all give a special salute to everyone

who is fighting in this race?

We are so proud of each one of you

And remember you are covered in God's grace.

Breaking the Silence

We can't physically feel your pain, so we don't know exactly what you go through

Please know that we are here, we care, and our hearts go out to you.

So, let's remember to not only show our support

But also offer a little guidance.

And we can do them both continuing to "Break the Silence".

You are not alone

Some days mays seen real ruff

and it seems like everyone is gone

I just want to assure you

that you are never alone.

Jesus will always be here

To guide you and give you comfort

He is the only one who is able to

Give you unconditional support

When the tuff times hit you

and it seems like everyone else is moving on

but it's kind of hard for you

because you're getting tired of being strong

You must stop depending on your self

And give your cares to Jesus Christ

He will fight your battles

and He will also be your light.

Know that my prayers are with you

So, continue to lead your home.

And even if it appears a certain way

Always remember "You are not alone".

Jesus is Love

We all look forward to celebrating Valentine's Day

We want to show our family and friends love, in a special way.

I think of what we all do to show how much we care.

We buy jewelry, candy, balloons or maybe a teddy bear.

We so often miss the real meaning of love,

forgetting that it starts with our father above.

The Holy Bible explains Love plain and clear

But we must walk in the spirit so we can hear.

Love is patient and kind, trust and hopes for the best.

Love is not rude, even during a test.

Love is not in it to only please self

And it does not brag if it comes into wealth.

Love isn't walking around looking mean with a frown.

And you best believe it doesn't like to see others down.

Love does not continue to bring up the past.

Love never fails, True love will last.

Jesus really wants us to love one another.

So, let's examine ourselves so we can please our father.

Not just for today, but let's implement it in our life.

So, we won't look like darkness but instead shine like a light.

About the Author

Melinda Green Carpenter has been writing poetry as a form of coping, encouraging, expressing love, spreading awareness and witnessing ever since she was a child. She has spoken at several awareness events, church programs, weddings, funerals and family functions. She is skilled at teaching people who is battling mental illness ways to use poetry as a form of coping. Also, she teaches the youth at her church as a way of using art to give glory to God. She is a person who has battled with addiction, depression, loss, vitiligo (a skin condition) and so many other adversaries.

Melinda serves in her community as much as she can, merely out of love for others. Melinda resides in Moundville, Alabama with her husband Keith and their daughter Aleese.

Made in the USA
Columbia, SC
12 June 2025